DeepSeek

Exploring the Future of Intelligent Systems

Taylor Royce

DEDICATION

To the visionaries, the trailblazers, and the unrelenting information seekers.

To those who have the courage to test the limits of what is feasible, who eagerly and resolutely confront the unknown.

To the innovators influencing the direction of technology and the common people whose lives it changes.

And to my friends, family, and mentors, whose constant encouragement and support have served as my cornerstone

It's your work. May it encourage, test, and help create a future where technology and human potential coexist peacefully.

DISCLAIMER

This book is meant solely for educational and informational purposes. Although every attempt has been made to guarantee accuracy, completeness, and relevance, the publisher and author offer no explicit or implicit guarantees about the information's application.

Since the field of artificial intelligence (AI) is developing quickly, some ideas, tools, or laws may eventually become obsolete. The information presented should not be interpreted as technical, legal, financial, or other professional advice. Before making judgments based on the information in this book, readers are urged to carry out independent research and speak with knowledgeable professionals.

Any liability for incidental, consequential, direct, or indirect damages arising from the use, misuse, or interpretation of the material provided is disclaimed by the publisher and author. Any mentions of particular businesses, innovations, or goods are merely meant to serve as examples and do not imply affiliations or endorsements.

Furthermore, different governments have different ethical standards and legal frameworks pertaining to AI. When creating, using, or dealing with AI systems, readers should be aware of and abide by the relevant rules and regulations.

All company names, product names, and trademarks listed in this book are the property of their respective owners. No copyright violation is meant.

You understand and accept the terms stated in this disclaimer by reading this book.

CONTENTS

ACKNOWLEDGMENTS

It would not have been possible to finish this book without the help, advice, and contributions of several people and organizations.

I want to start by expressing my sincere gratitude to my family and friends, whose constant support and faith in my idea kept me going along this journey. I sincerely appreciate all of your help, which has been priceless.

Additionally, I want to thank the artificial intelligence community's thought leaders, developers, and researchers. The groundwork for this book was laid by their innovative work and unwavering quest for creativity. The AI community's cumulative knowledge and advances continue to impact the future, and I am delighted to contribute to this continuing conversation.

I would especially like to thank the professionals, mentors, and coworkers who evaluated my work, offered helpful criticism, and shared their perspectives. Your knowledge and well-considered recommendations have improved the content, guaranteeing its breadth, precision, and applicability.

We appreciate your interest in and readiness to learn more about the large and developing field of artificial intelligence, readers. Your involvement with these concepts is what propels significant advancements in the industry, regardless of your role—researcher, developer, company leader, or just enthusiast.

Lastly, I want to express my gratitude for the technological resources and instruments that enabled the creation of this book. The same topic covered in these pages has been validated by the capacity to use AI-driven tools, communicate remotely, and access a wealth of knowledge.

This book is the result of shared ambition and group learning. I want to express my gratitude to everyone who has contributed, no matter how tiny.

CHAPTER 1

OVERVIEW OF DEEPSEEK AI

DeepSeek AI, which combines cutting-edge machine learning methods with complex natural language processing models, is a major advancement in artificial intelligence. Knowing the technology underlying AI is becoming more and more important as it continues to permeate daily life. This chapter provides an overview of DeepSeek AI, including its history, goals, salient characteristics, and influence on the larger AI field.

1.1 The Development of DeepSeek AI and the Evolution of AI

From basic rule-based systems to extremely complex deep learning models that can reason like humans, artificial intelligence has experienced a dramatic metamorphosis. The evolution of AI can be divided into a number of important phases:

1. **Rule-Based Systems:** Earlier AI was based on clearly written rules, which limited its adaptability and necessitated a great deal of human involvement.

2. **Machine Learning:** Without the need for human rule-setting, robots can now learn from data thanks to the development of statistical algorithms.

3. The creation of neural networks, especially deep learning models, allowed machines to absorb complex data, identify patterns, and produce text and images that resembled those of humans. This was the third revolution in deep learning.

4. **Transformer-Based AI:** Natural language processing was transformed with the advent of transformer models, such Google's BERT and OpenAI's GPT series. These models showed previously unheard-of talents in text production and comprehension.

5. **The Arrival of DeepSeek AI:** DeepSeek AI is built on these developments and aims to expand the possibilities of artificial intelligence. To provide state-of-the-art AI solutions, it combines sophisticated transformer topologies, big training datasets, and performance-optimized tactics.

DeepSeek AI is unique because it can process large volumes of text material, comprehend context more deeply, and produce incredibly well-reasoned and contextually appropriate solutions.

1.2 Comprehending the Function and Potential of DeepSeek AI

DeepSeek AI's main objective is to develop an AI model that can help in a variety of domains, from automation and research to innovative problem-solving. With a wide range of features, it is a flexible tool for companies, developers, educators, and everyday consumers.

Primary Skills

- **Natural Language Understanding (NLU):** DeepSeek AI is useful for conversational AI, customer service, and virtual assistants because it can understand difficult inquiries.
- **material Generation:** DeepSeek AI is capable of producing excellent written material in a variety of

fields, from writing essays to writing code snippets.

- **Code Assistance:** AI-assisted coding, debugging, and optimization saves developers time and increases productivity.

- **Data Analysis and Insights:** DeepSeek AI can summarize important information, extract insights, and facilitate data-driven decision-making by processing large datasets.

- **Creative Applications:** The AI can help with poetry, screenplays, brainstorming, and other creative tasks.

Because of its wide range of capabilities, DeepSeek AI is an effective tool in both academic and professional contexts.

1.3 DeepSeek AI's Main Features and Developments

DeepSeek AI has a number of innovations that set it apart from previous AI models.

1.3.1 Neural Network Based on Transformers

Transformers, a ground-breaking deep learning framework

that makes it possible to process massive datasets in an efficient and scalable manner, form the foundation of DeepSeek AI's architecture. These networks promote contextual awareness by weighing the significance of various words and phrases in a sentence using self-attention mechanisms.

1.3.2 Training Data on a Large Scale

A huge corpus of text from a variety of sources, such as books, scholarly journals, open-source repositories, and internet information, is used to train the AI. The model can accurately reply to a wide range of topics because of the large amount of training data.

1.3.3 Reinforcement Learning with Human Feedback (RLHF) and Self-Supervised Learning

DeepSeek AI uses self-supervised learning to identify patterns and connections in data without the need for explicit labels. Furthermore, by ensuring that the AI is in line with human values and preferences, reinforcement learning with human feedback (RLHF) improves the quality and dependability of responses.

1.3.4 Advanced Strategies for Optimization

The model uses a number of optimization strategies, such as:

- **Model Pruning:** Cutting off extraneous parameters without sacrificing functionality.
- **Quantization:** Reducing the accuracy of non-critical computations to reduce computing demands.
- **Efficient Parallel Processing:** To increase response time, tasks are divided among several GPUs and TPUs.

DeepSeek AI can now achieve great performance with minimal processing overhead thanks to these improvements.

1.4 DeepSeek AI's Effect on AI Advancement and Society

DeepSeek AI is a noteworthy advancement in AI that has an impact on a number of sectors and societal areas.

1.4.1 Revolutionizing Sectors

DeepSeek AI has the potential to transform several

industries:

- **Healthcare:** Helping with medical research, making individualized health suggestions, and detecting ailments.

- **Finance:** Trading strategy optimization, fraud detection, and automated financial analysis.

- **Education:** Helping with academic research, tutoring pupils, and improving individualized learning experiences.

- **Software Development:** Offering aid with software documentation, debugging support, and real-time coding recommendations.

1.4.2 AI Safety and Ethical Considerations

Ensuring ethical use and reducing potential hazards are essential as AI grows in strength. DeepSeek AI has tools to combat prejudice, stop false information, and improve equity. To ensure responsible AI deployment, ethical AI governance frameworks are being actively deployed.

1.5 DeepSeek AI's Future

Opportunities for additional DeepSeek AI improvements

are presented by the ongoing progress of AI. Current studies concentrate on:

- **Improving Model Efficiency:** Cutting down on computational expenses and energy usage.
- The integration of AI with images, audio, and video to improve user engagement is known as "Expanding Multimodal Capabilities."
- The goal of Developing More Explainable AI is to increase user trust by making AI decision-making more transparent.

DeepSeek AI is anticipated to be crucial in determining the direction of artificial intelligence and human-machine cooperation as the field develops.

In order to prepare for a more thorough examination of DeepSeek AI's architecture and features in the following chapters, this chapter offers a thorough overview of the technology.

CHAPTER 2

DEEPSEEK AI'S ARCHITECTURE

At the forefront of artificial intelligence, DeepSeek AI uses state-of-the-art architectures to propel improvements in machine learning, natural language processing, and general AI capabilities. This chapter offers a thorough examination of DeepSeek AI's core architecture, outlining the essential elements that make up its structure, the training techniques it uses, and the tactics it employs to maximize performance. It also looks at the issues surrounding AI bias and the steps being made to improve fairness in outputs produced by AI.

2.1 Model Architecture: The Operation of DeepSeek AI

Transformers, a cutting-edge deep learning framework that has transformed artificial intelligence since its debut in the 2017 paper "Attention Is All You Need" by Vaswani et al., forms the basis of DeepSeek AI's architecture. The majority of cutting-edge AI models, such as DeepSeek AI, are supported by the transformer architecture, which enables them to analyze enormous volumes of data effectively and provide replies that are remarkably accurate and coherent and human-like.

Important Elements of the Model Architecture of DeepSeek AI

The transformer model is composed of encoder-decoder layers, each of which has numerous feedforward and self-attention layers. See Transformers and Self-Attention Mechanism.

- **Self-attention** enables the model to capture long-range dependencies that conventional recurrent neural networks (RNNs) have trouble with by weighing the relative value of various words in a phrase.
- The model may concentrate on several facets of the input data at once thanks to multi-head attention methods, which enhance contextual comprehension.

Positional Encoding and Token Embeddings

- Transformers do not necessarily handle input in the same order as sequential models. By giving each token's location within a sequence a distinct numerical representation, positional encoding enables the model to comprehend word order.
- Token embeddings maintain the semantic linkages between words or subwords while transforming them into vector representations in a high-dimensional space.

Layer normalization and Feedforward Neural Networks (FFNNs)

- Each transformer block has fully connected feedforward networks that process data before sending it to the following layer.
- By normalizing activations, layer normalization prevents problems like vanishing or exploding gradients and guarantees stability in training.

Large-Scale Model Parameters DeepSeek AI is a large language model (LLM) that necessitates significant computational resources because of its billions of parameters.

The model retains its general knowledge skills while adapting to particular applications through the use of pre-training and fine-tuning.

2.2 Algorithms and Training Data

DeepSeek AI's precision and efficiency are a result of the use of advanced learning techniques and massive-scale training on different datasets. To ensure resilience, training AI models of this size necessitates rigorous algorithmic procedures and meticulous data source curation.

Sources of Training Data

High-quality content from openly accessible websites, scholarly publications, books, and news sources is known as "web scraped data."

- Curated datasets acquired through collaborations with publications and organizations are referred to as Licensed and Proprietary Datasets.
- User Interaction Data: Model responses are improved and errors are decreased through feedback loops from actual interactions.

Important Training Methods

In contrast to standard supervised learning, which necessitates labeled datasets, self-supervised learning enables the model to produce pertinent outputs or forecast textual segments that are missing based on patterns discovered during training. As a result, DeepSeek AI can scale more effectively and enhance its cross-domain generalization capabilities.

The training of DeepSeek AI relies heavily on Reinforcement Learning with Human Feedback (RLHF). In order to make the model match human expectations, human evaluators rank AI-generated responses. The AI's capacity to produce ethical and contextually relevant replies is improved by this approach.

Fine-Tuning on Domain-Specific Data

- DeepSeek AI is fine-tuned to specialize in fields like finance, law, and medical after being pre-trained on general datasets.
- Businesses can implement AI solutions that are

suited to their sector's requirements through custom fine-tuning.

DeepSeek AI is built to learn from fresh data over time, guaranteeing that it stays current with the most recent information. This is achieved through continuous learning and adaptive updates.

- It develops in tandem with advances in technology and human knowledge thanks to this adaptive learning framework.

2.3 Performance Optimization Techniques

Optimizing DeepSeek AI's performance is crucial to lowering computational costs and improving efficiency because of its enormous scale. To balance speed, accuracy, and performance, a number of tactics are used.

Methods of Optimization

The training of DeepSeek AI necessitates the parallel operation of thousands of Graphics Processing Units (GPUs) and TPUs (Tensor Processing Units) Efficient

Training with Distributed Computing.

- Training time is greatly decreased by model parallelism and data parallelism, which divide computations among several machines.

Quantization and Pruning

- **Quantization** drastically reduces memory use without sacrificing accuracy by reducing the precision of model weights from 32-bit floating point numbers to 8-bit integers.
- Pruning simplifies the model while preserving necessary features by eliminating unnecessary parameters.

The Mixture of Experts (MoE) Approach dynamically chooses specific groups of neurons rather than activating all model parameters for each job, lowering computing load without sacrificing performance.

Caching and Precomputed Embeddings.

The model can produce answers more quickly thanks to precomputed embeddings for frequently used words and phrases.

Adaptive Tokenization

- This method improves accuracy and speed for many languages and situations by dynamically modifying the input structure rather than processing words in fixed-length chunks.

2.4 Addressing Prejudice and Enhancing Equity

Addressing bias and fairness is essential as AI systems grow more ingrained in daily life in order to avoid ethical issues and guarantee that AI helps all users equally. To identify, reduce, and eliminate biases in its responses, DeepSeek AI uses a variety of approaches.

Bias in AI Challenges

- **Data Imbalance:** The model may propagate prejudices if training data is biased toward particular groups or viewpoints.
- **Historical Prejudices:** AI that has been trained on historical data may exhibit societal prejudices that have been documented in the past.

- **Contextual Ambiguities:** AI may inadvertently pick up implicit biases from certain linguistic patterns.

Methods for Mitigating Bias

1. Representative and Diverse Training Data

- Datasets are meticulously selected to encompass a variety of cultures, views, and points of view.
- Before training starts, bias detection algorithms examine datasets to identify any possible imbalances.

2. Fairness-Aware Algorithms

- Ethical AI frameworks guarantee that model outputs fairly represent underrepresented groups.
- Biased linguistic patterns are eliminated by introducing Bias-correction layers.

3. Human-in-the-Loop Evaluation

- Groups of specialists in AI ethics review and audit model results on a regular basis.
- Mechanisms for user feedback enable real-time corrections to lessen biases.

4. Transparency and Explainability

- DeepSeek AI has explainability features that let users know why a particular output was produced.
- The implementation of fairness interventions is documented in transparency reports.

5. Regulatory Compliance

- The model complies with international AI ethical guidelines, including the U.S. AI Policy frameworks and the EU AI Act.
- Collaborations with academic institutions aid in the improvement of fairness techniques by drawing on empirical data.

The foundation of DeepSeek AI is a strong transformer-based architecture that uses large-scale deep learning methods and self-attention mechanisms to provide AI-generated responses of superior quality. To continuously improve its performance, its training approach combines large datasets, self-supervised learning, and reinforcement learning. Quantization, pruning, and distributed computing are some optimization techniques that guarantee the model's efficiency while preserving its cutting-edge capabilities.

Additionally, DeepSeek AI is developed in accordance with ethical AI principles, which guarantees that it reduces prejudices and fosters justice. The model aims to be as impartial and equitable as feasible by utilizing a combination of diverse training data, fairness-aware algorithms, and human-in-the-loop evaluations.

More powerful, responsible, and human-aligned artificial intelligence solutions will be made possible by the advancement of DeepSeek AI's architecture and techniques as AI continues to develop.

CHAPTER 3

DEEPSEEK AI'S NATURAL LANGUAGE PROCESSING CAPABILITIES

The foundation of DeepSeek AI's capabilities is Natural Language Processing (NLP), which allows it to intelligently comprehend, produce, and interact with human language. DeepSeek AI is a potent tool for applications ranging from content creation to real-time translation and conversational AI since it uses cutting-edge deep learning algorithms to parse text with amazing precision.

This chapter explores the ways in which DeepSeek AI generates and summarizes text, supports many languages, analyzes context and semantics, and powers chatbots and virtual assistants.

3.1 Contextual and Semantic Understanding

Understanding context and semantics is one of the core problems in natural language processing. Because human language is so complex, words and sentences can have multiple meanings depending on the situation. DeepSeek AI uses a number of cutting-edge strategies to tackle this problem.

3.1.1 Language Models Based on Transformers

The transformer architecture at the core of DeepSeek AI allows it to process entire text sequences instead of just analyzing individual words. The model can assess the relative relevance of various words in a phrase thanks to the self-attention mechanism, which guarantees a more thorough comprehension of context.

Take the following line, for instance:
- He went to the bank to withdraw money.
- She stood on the river bank, watching the boats."

It could be difficult for a simple language model to distinguish between "bank" as a riverbank and "bank" as a financial organization. DeepSeek AI, on the other hand, deduces the correct meaning by examining the surrounding words.

3.1.2 Semantic Relationships and Contextual Embeddings

Contextual word embeddings, in which a word's meaning changes according to its context, are used by DeepSeek AI. Contextual embeddings provide dynamic interpretations, in contrast to conventional word vectors that give each word a single meaning.

Furthermore, DeepSeek AI creates semantic connections between words, phrases, and sentences to guarantee more precise answers in challenging language situations.

3.1.3 Managing Polysemy and Ambiguity

Probabilistic models that assess a word's several meanings and choose the best one depending on context are incorporated into DeepSeek AI. This skill is especially useful for applications like sentiment analysis, where a sophisticated grasp of language is necessary to identify sarcasm or inferred meaning.

3.2 Translation and Multilingual Capabilities

DeepSeek AI's multilingual capabilities enable smooth cross-linguistic communication by removing linguistic obstacles.

3.2.1 Translation using Neural Machines (NMT)

To produce high-quality translations between languages, DeepSeek AI uses sophisticated Neural Machine Translation (NMT) algorithms. NMT uses deep learning to provide natural and fluid translations, in contrast to rule-based translation systems that depend on preset grammatical rules.

3.2.2 Understanding Different Languages

DeepSeek AI can comprehend and produce information in numerous languages without the need for distinct models for each language, going beyond mere translation. The AI can learn verbal patterns across languages thanks to shared multilingual embeddings, which provide this functionality.

- For instance, DeepSeek AI can produce responses in any of these languages while preserving contextual coherence if it is trained on data in English, Spanish, and French.

DeepSeek AI's multilingual models allow for real-time language adaption, which makes it helpful for the following applications:

- **International customer service:** Translating consumer questions and answers automatically.
- Supporting multilingual teams is an example of international collaboration.
- **Language learning:** Offering contextual recommendations and grammar correction through AI-powered tutoring.

3.3 Summarization and Text Generation

The text generation and summarization capabilities of DeepSeek AI have important uses in automation, research, and content production.

3.3.1 Text Generation Driven by AI

DeepSeek AI can produce human-like writing in a variety of formats by utilizing deep learning, including:

- **Blog entries and articles:** Helping authors by creating excellent material.
- The creation of organized documentation for software, research, and business reports is known as "technical documentation."
- **Creative writing:** Using AI-generated storylines to assist poets, screenwriters, and novelists.

DeepSeek AI uses the following techniques to guarantee coherence and relevance:

- **Prompt engineering:** Modifying input prompts to optimize the AI's output.
- Adjusting writing tone and style according to customer preferences is known as "style adaptation."

3.3.2 Methods of Summarization

Two primary forms of text summary are used by DeepSeek

AI:

- Selecting important sentences from the source material while maintaining meaning is known as "extractive summarization."
- The process of rewriting the content in a shortened format while encapsulating the main ideas of the original text in new terms is known as abstract summarization.

Text summarization is used in the following applications:

- **News aggregation:** Condensing daily news updates.
- **Academic research:** Getting long research articles down to size.
- **Legal and business documentation:** Taking important details out of reports, policies, and contracts.

3.3.3 Rewriting and Paraphrasing"

Content can be efficiently rewritten using DeepSeek AI while retaining its original meaning. This function is useful because

- The process of modifying articles for various

audiences is known as "content repurposing."

- Rewriting material using original wording is one way to avoid plagiarism.
- **Improving clarity:** Making difficult words easier to understand.

3.4 Conversational AI: Virtual Assistants and Chatbots

The conversational features of DeepSeek AI make it possible to create intelligent chatbots and virtual assistants that can engage with users in meaningful and natural ways.

3.4.1 NLP's Function in Conversational AI

The conversational AI models from DeepSeek AI use dialogue management systems and natural language understanding (NLU) to:

- **Recognize user intent:** Determining the reason for an inquiry.
- **Maintain context:** Recalling previous exchanges to guarantee cohesive discussions.
- **Produce suitable answers:** Formulating answers according to the conversation's circumstances.

3.4.2 Automation of Customer Support

Companies automate customer interactions with DeepSeek AI to improve service efficiency and response times. Frequently asked inquiries (FAQs) can be handled by AI-powered customer service.

- Offer aid with troubleshooting.
- When required, escalate complicated matters to human representatives.

3.4.3 AI Personal Helpers

As a personal assistant, DeepSeek AI can aid users with duties such

- **Appointment scheduling:** Calendar management and reminder setup.
- **Offering recommendations:** Making recommendations for films, books, or merchandise.
- **Responding to general knowledge queries:** Acting as a repository of information for brief queries.

3.4.4 Improving Conversations That Feel Human

DeepSeek AI enhances its capacity for human-like dialogue through ongoing training and reinforcement learning. The following methods are employed to improve the quality of interactions:

- Sentiment analysis is the process of identifying emotional tones and modifying reactions appropriately.

- **Context retention:** Preserving recollection of previous exchanges during a session.

- **Multi-turn dialogues:** Handling lengthy discussions with well-reasoned answers.

DeepSeek AI is a potent tool for text generation, understanding, and engagement because of its natural language processing skills. It is essential in a variety of domains, including business, education, content creation, and customer service, because of its capacity to comprehend context, support various languages, produce high-quality material, and power conversational AI.

The future of human-AI communication will be greatly influenced by DeepSeek AI's developments in natural language processing (NLP), which will make interactions more intelligent, smooth, and efficient as AI develops.

CHAPTER 4

DeepSeek AI in Industry Applications

With previously unheard-of levels of automation, accuracy, and efficiency, artificial intelligence has completely transformed a number of industries. Leading this change with its sophisticated machine learning and natural language processing (NLP) skills is DeepSeek AI. DeepSeek AI is helping enterprises make data-driven decisions, increase productivity, and improve user experiences across a range of industries, including healthcare, finance, education, and business operations.

This chapter examines the applications of DeepSeek AI in important sectors, describing its function in corporate automation, healthcare, finance, and education.

4.1 AI in Healthcare: Drug Discovery and Diagnosis

Significant improvements in medication development,

treatment suggestions, and disease detection have resulted from the application of AI in healthcare. Large volumes of medical data may be processed by DeepSeek AI thanks to its strong natural language processing and deep learning capabilities, which offer researchers and medical professionals insightful information.

4.1.1 Diagnostics Driven by AI

DeepSeek AI analyzes imaging data (such as MRIs, CT scans, and X-rays), lab results, and patient information to improve diagnostic accuracy.

By identifying abnormalities, machine learning models trained on medical datasets might assist physicians in making earlier and more precise diagnoses of ailments including cancer, heart disease, and neurological problems.

AI-assisted diagnostics improve patient outcomes by lowering human error and giving doctors a second perspective.

4.1.2 Customized Treatment Plans and Predictive Healthcare

DeepSeek AI examines lifestyle factors, genetic markers, and patient history to forecast the course of a disease.

Based on a patient's unique health information, customized treatment plans can be developed, guaranteeing more successful interventions.

Preventive care measures are made possible by AI models' ability to detect patients who are at high risk of developing diseases like diabetes, stroke, or heart disease.

4.1.3 Drug Development and Discovery

AI predicts possible medication candidates and analyzes molecular structures to speed up drug discovery.

To find novel treatment strategies, DeepSeek AI analyzes academic articles, clinical trial data, and biomedical literature.

AI-powered simulations speed up approvals and patient access to life-saving treatments by cutting down on the time and expense of creating new drugs.

4.2 AI in Finance: Market Analysis and Fraud Detection

AI has been adopted by the financial sector to improve client experiences, optimize investment strategies, and strengthen security. DeepSeek AI is a priceless tool in the financial industry because of its real-time processing and interpretation capabilities of massive datasets.

4.2.1 Risk assessment and fraud detection

Artificial intelligence (AI)-driven fraud detection systems examine transactional data to spot odd trends and highlight possible fraudulent activity.

In order to stop credit card fraud, identity theft, and money laundering, DeepSeek AI uses machine learning algorithms to identify irregularities in financial transactions.

Financial organizations use AI to assess risk, more accurately determining loan eligibility and credit scores.

4.2.2 Predictive analytics and market analysis

To provide financial suggestions, AI models examine historical data, news sentiment, and stock market patterns.

By improving algorithmic trading, DeepSeek AI empowers traders to make data-driven choices based on current market conditions.

Financial analysts use sentiment research to determine how the general public is responding to business earnings releases, economic events, and geopolitical developments.

4.2.3 AI-Powered Banking Customer Support

DeepSeek AI-powered chatbots offer consumers immediate support by answering questions about loan applications, account balances, and financial planning.

AI-powered financial advisors provide individualized investment plans according to the risk tolerance and preferences of the user.

Automated compliance monitoring lowers legal risks by ensuring financial firms follow regulations.

4.3 AI in Education: Tutoring and Personalized Learning

AI-driven technologies are improving learning experiences for both teachers and students as education undergoes a digital revolution. Personalized tutoring, automated grading systems, and adaptive learning platforms all heavily rely on DeepSeek AI.

4.3.1 Tailored Educational Journeys

Learning routes are tailored by DeepSeek AI according to each student's learning style, learning pace, and areas of strength and weakness.

AI is used by adaptive learning platforms to provide activities and study guides based on user preferences.

Without having to wait for teacher assessments, students can get immediate feedback that helps them get better in particular subject areas.

4.3.2 AI-Powered Virtual Classrooms and Tutoring

AI instructors offer immediate clarifications and detailed solutions for challenging issues in disciplines like physics, math, and programming.

DeepSeek AI-powered virtual classrooms improve distance learning by enabling engaging discussions and providing real-time answers to student questions.

Apps for language learning use AI to improve grammar, check pronunciation, and simulate conversations.

4.3.3 Automatic Evaluation and Grading

DeepSeek AI saves teachers a great deal of time by automating the grading of essays, assignments, and multiple-choice exams.

NLP models provide helpful criticism by assessing written comments for coherence, grammar, and relevance.

By spotting plagiarized text from internet sources,

AI-powered plagiarism detection programs protect academic integrity.

4.4 AI in Business: Increasing Productivity and Automating Workflows

AI is being used by companies in a variety of sectors to improve consumer experiences, expedite processes, and make better decisions. The automated features of DeepSeek AI assist businesses in cutting expenses, increasing productivity, and spurring creativity.

4.4.1 Process Optimization and Workflow Automation

Data input, scheduling, and customer service are among the repetitious duties that AI automates.

Robotic process automation (RPA) driven by DeepSeek AI increases efficiency by reducing the need for human intervention in repetitive tasks.

AI-driven analytics are used by businesses to improve logistics, inventory tracking, and supply chain management.

4.4.2 Increasing Worker Efficiency

Virtual assistants driven by AI do administrative duties, freeing up staff members to concentrate on higher-value work.

Smart document processing solutions reduce human labor by analyzing emails, reports, and contracts to extract important information.

By creating reports, summarizing meetings, and making project recommendations, DeepSeek AI makes cooperation easier.

4.4.3 AI in Customer Engagement and Marketing

AI-powered chatbots answer consumer questions, offering prompt answers and tailored suggestions.

By analyzing consumer behavior and preferences, DeepSeek AI assists companies in developing marketing campaigns that are specifically targeted.

Sentiment analysis tools evaluate how consumers view brands, enabling businesses to improve their approach.

By utilizing cutting-edge AI and NLP skills to enhance productivity, security, and user experiences, DeepSeek AI is revolutionizing several sectors. It helps with medication discovery and diagnostics in the healthcare industry and improves market analysis and fraud detection in the financial sector. AI-driven individualized learning helps education, and automation helps businesses streamline processes and boost output.

DeepSeek AI will become even more important in influencing these sectors' futures as AI technology develops further, spurring innovation and opening up new avenues for exploration.

CHAPTER 5

DEEPSEEK AI AND COMPUTER VISION

Within artificial intelligence, computer vision is a revolutionary field that allows machines to comprehend and evaluate visual information. With its breakthroughs in deepfake detection, autonomous systems, medical imaging, and sophisticated image and video recognition, DeepSeek AI has pushed innovation in a variety of industries.

This chapter examines DeepSeek AI's capabilities in computer vision, describing how it improves object detection, advances robotics and self-driving cars, advances medical diagnostics, and poses ethical questions with AI-generated media.

5.1 Capabilities for Image and Video Recognition

DeepSeek AI mimics how people detect and interpret images by processing and comprehending visual input using deep learning algorithms. Many applications, such as automatic content filtering and security surveillance, rely on this feature.

5.1.1 Detection and Classification of Objects

DeepSeek AI uses convolutional neural networks (CNNs) to recognize and classify items in photos and videos.

Advanced models such as Faster R and YOLO (You Only Look Once)-CNNs allow for highly accurate real-time object detection.

Applications include consumer applications such as smart home appliances, industrial automation, and traffic monitoring.

5.1.2 Technology for Facial Recognition

AI-powered facial recognition improves security in personal gadgets, banks, and airports by mapping face traits to confirm identities.

DeepSeek AI improves facial recognition algorithms to increase accuracy in a variety of occlusions, angles, and lighting situations.

Discussions on regulatory oversight have been sparked by worries about bias and privacy in facial recognition models.

5.1.3 Autonomous Scene Understanding and Navigation

AI helps with robotics and autonomous driving by interpreting road conditions, pedestrian motions, and obstructions.

To improve machine vision, DeepSeek AI combines motion tracking, depth perception, and image segmentation.

AI-based navigation is used by delivery robots and drones to optimize routes and avoid obstacles.

5.2 AI in Robotics and Autonomous Vehicles

To navigate complicated settings, autonomous systems rely on perception, decision-making, and control mechanisms driven by artificial intelligence. DeepSeek AI is essential to the development of robotic automation and self-driving technology.

5.2.1 Technologies for Self-Driving Cars

LiDAR, radar, and cameras are among the AI-powered sensors that offer real-time environmental mapping.

This data is processed by DeepSeek AI to identify possible hazards, road signs, and lane markings.

Adaptive cruise control and vehicle trajectory prediction are made possible by end-to-end deep learning algorithms.

5.2.2 Industrial Automation and Robotics

Robotic arms powered by AI in production lines maximize accuracy, speed, and security.

Robots can now identify and control items in dynamic

surroundings thanks to DeepSeek AI.

Drones with AI capabilities support disaster relief, construction site surveillance, and agriculture.

5.2.3 Assistive AI and Human-Robot Interaction

AI enhances human-robot cooperation in sectors like logistics and healthcare.

Exoskeletons driven by DeepSeek AI help those with limited mobility.

AI-powered warehouse robots expedite order fulfillment and inventory control.

5.3 AI-Assisted Diagnosis and Medical Imaging

One of the most significant uses of AI in healthcare is medical imaging, which helps physicians identify and diagnose illnesses more precisely. Diagnostic screening, pathology, and radiography are all improved by DeepSeek AI.

5.3.1 AI in Imaging Analysis and Radiology

DeepSeek AI examines CT, MRI, and X-ray images to find anomalies like cancers and fractures.

AI-assisted radiography enhances early disease identification and lowers diagnostic mistakes.

Over time, AI models improve diagnostic accuracy by learning from large medical datasets.

5.3.2 Predictive analytics and disease detection

AI recognizes patterns in medical photos that could point to neurological conditions, cardiovascular problems, or cancer.

Physicians can evaluate the course of a disease and the efficacy of treatment with the use of predictive analytics.

AI-powered solutions help radiologists in complicated circumstances by offering second opinions.

5.3.3 AI-Powered Microscopic Analysis and Pathology

DeepSeek AI detects malignant cells with high precision by automating biopsy slide analysis.

AI-powered microscopes aid in the diagnosis of infectious diseases including malaria and tuberculosis.

AI speeds up treatment decisions by cutting down on the amount of time needed for manual evaluation.

5.4 Ethical Challenges and Deepfake Technology

Opportunities and moral conundrums are presented by the emergence of deepfake technology, which is driven by artificial intelligence-generated synthetic media. Leading the way in identifying and reducing the hazards connected to AI-generated material is DeepSeek AI.

5.4.1 Deepfake Technology Understanding

Generative adversarial networks (GANs) are used in deepfakes to produce incredibly lifelike spoof photos and videos.

Artificial intelligence algorithms create convincing but misleading media by manipulating voices and facial expressions.

Applications include marketing, entertainment, identity theft, and disinformation campaigns.

5.4.2 Security Issues and Hazards

Cybersecurity is being threatened by deepfake frauds, which make financial fraud and identity theft possible.

Misinformation produced by AI propagates erroneous narratives, affecting public opinion and politics.

Consent, data privacy, and the possible abuse of AI in propaganda are ethical issues.

5.4.3 AI-Powered Identification and Control

To detect corrupted media, DeepSeek AI creates deepfake

detection models.

Artificial intelligence (AI)-driven methods for authenticity authentication examine irregularities in pixel patterns and facial movements.

The goal of AI governance plans and regulatory frameworks is to lessen the abuse of synthetic content.

By facilitating picture and video recognition, developing autonomous systems, enhancing medical diagnostics, and tackling the issues of deepfake technology, DeepSeek AI's computer vision capabilities are reshaping industries. The ethical implications of AI's applications must be carefully regulated as it develops to ensure responsible and advantageous use in all industries.

CHAPTER 6

DeepSeek AI's Function in Research and Development

By speeding up discoveries, streamlining intricate studies, and identifying patterns that humans could take decades to see, artificial intelligence is transforming research and development (R&D). From basic studies in physics, chemistry, and biology to extensive applications in space exploration, climate science, and human-AI cooperation, DeepSeek AI is essential to many scientific fields.

This chapter examines the ways in which DeepSeek AI promotes a collaborative research ecosystem, advances astronomical discoveries, mitigates the effects of climate change, and advances scientific innovation.

6.1 AI in Discovery and Scientific Research

Finding patterns, testing hypotheses, and gathering data

have long been the main goals of scientific inquiry. By automating data processing, forecasting results, and even developing new ideas based on enormous datasets, DeepSeek AI speeds up this process.

6.1.1 AI in Material Science and Physics

AI-powered simulations eliminate the need for expensive tests by enabling researchers to investigate novel materials at the atomic level.

DeepSeek AI optimizes algorithms that solve intricate physical equations, hence improving quantum computing.

In order to find possible new particles or interactions, machine learning algorithms examine particle physics data from experiments such as those carried out at CERN.

6.1.2 AI in Drug Discovery and Chemistry

AI models speed up materials engineering and drug development by forecasting chemical reactions and molecular characteristics.

By examining chemical structures and modeling how they interact with biological targets, DeepSeek AI finds possible medicinal molecules.

AI-driven automation in laboratories greatly increases R&D efficiency by cutting down on the amount of time needed for chemical synthesis and testing.

6.1.3 AI in Genetics and Biological Research

DeepSeek AI advances precision medicine by analyzing genetic data to find genes linked to illnesses.

AI-driven protein structure prediction is transforming medication development and illness research, as demonstrated by innovations like AlphaFold.

DeepSeek AI helps with synthetic biology by simulating the effects of genetic changes on cellular function.

6.2 AI for Sustainability and Climate Change

One of the biggest problems of our day is climate change, and artificial intelligence is essential to comprehending and lessening its impacts. DeepSeek AI supports sustainable behaviors, energy efficiency, and climate model analysis.

6.2.1 Climate Modeling Driven by AI

By uncovering hidden patterns in weather and climate oscillations, artificial intelligence (AI) improves the accuracy of traditional climate models, which rely on enormous volumes of historical data.

In order to help governments and organizations prepare for storms, wildfires, and droughts, DeepSeek AI enhances forecasting of extreme weather occurrences.

Artificial intelligence (AI) simulations evaluate how human activity affects climate change and offer data-driven suggestions for policymakers.

6.2.2 AI in Optimizing Renewable Energy

By forecasting energy output depending on meteorological

conditions, DeepSeek AI maximizes the generation of solar and wind energy.

AI-driven grid management solutions lessen dependency on fossil fuels by balancing energy supply and demand.

AI-powered smart buildings lower overall carbon footprints by dynamically adjusting energy use.

6.2.3 AI for Conservation and Environmental Protection

AI-powered image identification aids in monitoring biodiversity loss, illicit fishing, and deforestation.

DeepSeek AI analyzes trends in animal migration and habitat changes to help conserve wildlife.

AI-powered water management solutions enhance waste minimization and resource allocation.

6.3 AI in Astronomy and Space Exploration

AI has emerged as a crucial tool for analyzing astronomical data, supporting planetary exploration, and looking for extraterrestrial life. The immensity of space poses significant obstacles for data processing. By interpreting the massive volume of data produced by telescopes, satellites, and space missions, DeepSeek AI greatly advances space study.

6.3.1 AI in Cosmology and Astrophysics

To find exoplanets, black holes, and other celestial objects, DeepSeek AI analyzes data from space telescopes.

By analyzing gravitational wave transmissions, AI models can reveal details about the nature of space-time.

Scientists can better understand the genesis and evolution of galaxies with the use of AI-powered simulations.

6.3.2 AI in Robotics and Space Missions

DeepSeek AI helps space probes navigate autonomously so they can adjust to unpredictably changing space conditions.

By enhancing object detection and decision-making skills, artificial intelligence (AI) improves robotic systems used in planetary exploration, such as the Mars rovers.

By optimizing spacecraft trajectories, AI-driven mission planning lowers fuel consumption and raises mission success rates.

6.3.3 Artificial Intelligence in the Pursuit of Extraterrestrial Life

Radio telescope transmissions are processed by DeepSeek AI, which separates possible extraterrestrial contact from human-caused interference.

Artificial intelligence (AI) models examine planetary atmospheres to find biosignatures that suggest extraterrestrial life may exist.

By sifting through enormous volumes of observational data, machine learning improves the identification of habitable exoplanets.

6.4 Collaborative AI: Strengthening the Synergy between Human-AI Research

The transition from AI as a tool to AI as a cooperative collaborator in the research process is one of the most important advancements in AI-powered research. Leading this movement is DeepSeek AI, which improves human-AI collaboration to spur innovation and discoveries.

6.4.1 Research Assistants using AI

Thousands of scholarly articles are scanned by AI-powered literature review systems, which then summarize the most important findings for scholars.

By automating data analysis, DeepSeek AI frees up academics from tedious work so they can concentrate on solving complicated problems.

AI-driven experiment design makes recommendations for the best practices based on the findings of earlier studies.

6.4.2 AI for Corporate and Academic Research

Platforms driven by AI make it easier for academics from different organizations and sectors to collaborate.

By expediting the cycles of discovery and product development, DeepSeek AI improves research and development in technology organizations.

Knowledge graphs powered by AI show the connections between scientific ideas, assisting researchers in discovering new research topics.

6.4.3 Ethical Issues in Research Driven by AI

Concerns around data bias and the transparency of AI-generated conclusions are raised by the use of AI into research.

To prevent skewed outcomes, researchers must make sure AI models are trained on representative and diverse datasets.

To control AI's influence on scientific and technical decision-making, ethical frameworks are required.

From speeding up scientific discoveries to improving climate research, space exploration, and collaborative knowledge creation, DeepSeek AI is revolutionizing research and development in a number of domains. AI will play a bigger part in R&D as it develops further, becoming a vital tool for scientists, engineers, and innovators everywhere. But as AI becomes more and more integrated into research, it is imperative to guarantee its ethical and responsible application, paving the way for a time when human and AI intelligence collaborate to advance knowledge.

CHAPTER 7

DeepSeek AI's Ethical Issues and Challenges

Significant ethical issues and concerns are brought up by artificial intelligence as it becomes more pervasive in society. Like other cutting-edge AI systems, DeepSeek AI has to handle issues with governance, employment disruption, privacy, prejudice, and fairness. This chapter delves deeply into these important topics, emphasizing the moral obligations of AI researchers, decision-makers, and society at large.

7.1 AI Prejudice and Equitable Decision-Making

Bias in decision-making is one of the most urgent issues in AI ethics. DeepSeek AI and other AI systems learn from past data, which may contain biases reflecting societal injustices. AI-driven choices have the potential to sustain prejudice and unjust treatment in fields including hiring, financing, law enforcement, and healthcare if these biases are not adequately controlled.

7.1.1 Understanding Bias in AI

- **Data Bias:** AI models may produce discriminating results because they rely on datasets that contain historical biases.

- **Algorithmic Bias:** Due to poor design, algorithms may inadvertently increase discrepancies even when presented with objective data.

- **User Bias**: AI programs that have been trained on user-generated material may pick up on biases that exist in the data.

7.1.2 Resolving Bias in AI Models

- **Representative and Diverse Datasets:** Making certain that AI models are trained on representative and balanced datasets that represent a range of demographics.

- Regularly checking AI models for biased decision-making and addressing discrepancies is known as "Bias Audits and Testing."

- **Transparency and Explainability:** Enabling users and regulators to evaluate the fairness of AI judgments by making them interpretable.
- **Human Oversight:** Maintaining human involvement in AI decision-making, particularly in crucial areas like criminal justice and employment.

To make sure AI systems like DeepSeek AI advance justice and social equity rather than exacerbate already-existing disparities, bias prevention is crucial.

7.2 Data Security and Privacy Issues

Large volumes of data are necessary for AI systems to operate efficiently, which raises questions around data security and user privacy. DeepSeek AI has to strike a careful balance between protecting sensitive data and personalizing.

7.2.1 Major Privacy Risks in AI

- **Mass Data Collection:** AI-powered systems gather a lot of user data, which raises the possibility of abuse or illegal access.

- **Re-identification Risks:** Personal information may occasionally be exposed through the re-identification of even anonymised datasets.

- **Surveillance and Tracking:** Intrusive surveillance can be achieved by utilizing AI-powered monitoring solutions.

7.2.2 Protecting Privacy and Security

- **Data Minimization:** Gathering just the information required to lower exposure risks.

- **Encryption and Secure Storage:** Using strong encryption techniques to safeguard user data.

- **User Consent and Control:** Providing users with control and openness over the use of their data.

- **Regulation Compliance:** Respecting international privacy regulations such as the CCPA and GDPR to guarantee legitimate data processing.

To gain the trust of users and authorities, DeepSeek AI needs to put in place robust security measures and moral data handling procedures.

7.3 AI and Employment in the Future

Concerns over job displacement and changes in the global workforce are raised by the quick development of AI-driven automation. Like other intelligent systems, DeepSeek AI has the potential to both provide new opportunities and replace existing professions.

7.3.1 Economic Shifts and Job Displacement

- **Automation of Repetitive Tasks:** AI can effectively manage repetitive tasks in sectors including data entry, manufacturing, and customer service.
- **Impact on Skilled Professions:** AI is becoming more and more capable of doing intricate jobs in the fields of finance, medicine, law, and the arts.
- **Widening Economic Inequality:** Lower-paid workers may be disproportionately impacted by job losses in some industries.

7.3.2 New Career Prospects in the AI Era

- **AI Development and Maintenance:** There is an increasing need for machine learning experts, data scientists, and AI engineers.

- **Human-AI Collaboration Roles:** There is a growing need for human-in-the-loop specialists and AI ethics officers, among other positions involving supervision of AI systems.

- **New Industries and Business Models:** AI facilitates innovation in domains such as digital education, smart infrastructure, and tailored treatment.

7.3.3 Adapting to the AI-Driven Economy

- **Reskilling and Upskilling:** Businesses and governments need to fund AI education and training initiatives.

- **Universal Basic Income (UBI) and Safety Nets:** Some legislators suggest UBI as a remedy for unemployment brought on by automation.

- **Redefining Productivity and Work:** AI has the potential to change the emphasis from traditional jobs to strategic and innovative human contributions.

A fair and sustainable transition to an AI-integrated economy is just as difficult as controlling job displacement.

7.4 AI Governance and Regulation

The need for ethical and legal frameworks to control the advancement and application of AI technology is increasing as it develops. The corporate sector, governments, and international organizations are attempting to create rules that encourage the safe use of AI.

7.4.1 AI Regulation Is Needed

- **Preventing Harm:** AI must not be applied to detrimental tasks like manipulating deepfakes, making biased decisions, or abusing surveillance.
- **Ensuring Accountability:** Businesses and developers need to answer for the effects of AI systems.
- **Standardizing Ethical AI Development:** Creating best practices for security, equity, and transparency in AI.

7.4.2 Global AI Policies and Frameworks

- **European Union's AI Act:** A legislative framework that places higher restrictions on high-risk AI by classifying AI applications according to risk levels.

- The AI policies of the United States: Regulations pertaining to innovation balance, security, and fairness are being investigated by the US government.

- **China's AI Governance:** China has implemented AI ethical legislation with a focus on data protection and social stability.

- **United Nations and AI Ethics:** To avoid abuse and guarantee worldwide alignment, the UN has urged for international collaboration on AI governance.

7.4.3 Ethical AI Development Practices

- **Human-Centered AI:** As opposed to replacing human capabilities, AI should augment them.

- **Transparency and Explainability:** Making sure AI judgments are comprehensible and responsible.

- **Fairness testing and bias auditing**: Performing routine assessments to stop discrimination.
- **AI for Social Good**: Promoting AI applications that help people, such medical research and climate modeling.

For AI to be implemented ethically and to promote innovation and economic progress, governance must change with it.

Like other sophisticated AI systems, DeepSeek AI has ethical issues that need to be properly handled. To guarantee that AI advances society rather than harms it, concerns like bias, privacy, job displacement, and regulation must be addressed proactively. We can build an ethical and sustainable AI-driven future by tackling these issues through equitable AI development, conscientious governance, and workforce adoption tactics.

CHAPTER 8

DEEPSEEK'S ROADMAP AND THE FUTURE OF AI

Artificial Intelligence (AI) is developing at a never-before-seen pace, changing economies, industries, and how people interact with technology. Discussions on the future, moral ramifications, and societal effects of increasingly complex AI systems have heated up. As one of the industry's top innovators, DeepSeek AI is vital to determining the direction of AI research.

By looking at new developments, the development of artificial general intelligence (AGI), the controversy around open-source versus proprietary AI models, and the wider effects of AI on society, this chapter investigates the future of AI.

8.1 Innovations and Trends in AI

Researchers and developers are constantly pushing the

limits of what machines can do in the rapidly changing field of artificial intelligence. The upcoming phase of AI research is anticipated to be characterized by many significant trends:

8.1.1 AI Architectures of the Next Generation

- **Multimodal AI:** Advanced, human-like interactions will result from future AI models that incorporate several data sources, including text, graphics, video, and sound.
- **Neuro-Symbolic AI:** Deep learning and symbolic reasoning combined to improve AI's ability to interpret logical rules and abstract concepts.
- By enabling models to learn from data without sending it to a central server, Federated Learning, a decentralized method of AI training, improves privacy.

8.1.2 AI-Driven Personalization

- AI will be essential to the development of hyper-individualized services in a variety of sectors, such as healthcare, finance, and education.

- To deliver more individualized suggestions, predictive analytics, and adaptive learning experiences, DeepSeek AI will make use of cutting-edge machine learning algorithms.

8.1.3 Ethical and Explainable AI

- The need for accountable, interpretable, and transparent AI systems is rising.
- AI-driven choices will continue to be impartial and intelligible thanks to strategies like model interpretability tools, fairness audits, and ethical AI frameworks.

DeepSeek AI will be able to improve its models and capabilities while resolving ethical issues thanks to these advancements, which will propel the next generation of AI research.

8.2 Artificial General Intelligence (AGI) Evolution

The creation of Artificial General Intelligence (AGI), a

system with human-like reasoning, learning, and adaptability across a variety of fields, is one of the most ambitious objectives of AI research. AGI seeks to demonstrate broad intelligence, akin to human cognition, since current AI is excellent at specialized tasks (narrow AI).

8.2.1 AGI's Roadmap

- **Scaling Deep Learning Models:** In certain tasks, large-scale neural networks, like DeepSeek AI, are getting closer to human-level comprehension as their complexity increases.
- In order for robots to remember previous encounters and apply knowledge in a flexible manner, artificial general intelligence (AGI) will need improved memory storage and logical reasoning skills.
- **Self-Supervised Learning:** AI models of the future will be able to learn with less assistance from humans and adjust to new datasets and surroundings on their own.

8.2.2 Difficulties in Reaching AGI

- **Computational Limitations:** AGI would necessitate enormous computational resources that are much beyond present capacity.

- **Alignment with Human Values:** One of the biggest challenges is making sure AGI is in line with moral standards and human values.

- **Control and Safety Measures:** If AGI growth is allowed to continue unchecked, it may have unexpected repercussions, which calls for strict safety measures.

Although artificial general intelligence (AGI) is still a theoretical idea, small steps in AI research are progressively closing the gap between narrow AI and more generalized intelligence. By improving algorithms that become more autonomous and flexible, DeepSeek AI is actively advancing these developments.

8.3 Proprietary vs. Open-Source AI Models

The balance between proprietary and open-source AI models is a significant topic of discussion in AI development. Every strategy includes pros and cons that affect the ethical implications, security, and accessibility of AI technologies.

8.3.1 Open-Source AI: Transparency and Collaboration

- **Accessibility:** By enabling researchers and developers to expand upon pre-existing frameworks, open-source AI promotes innovation.
- **Community-Driven Improvements:** Constant improvements, bug fixes, and security patches are the result of crowdsourced development.
- **Ethical Oversight:** Open-source AI is subject to public review, which helps guarantee that models continue to be impartial and responsible.

8.3.2 Proprietary AI: Commercialization and Competitive Advantage

- **Data Privacy and Security:** Stronger security measures can be put in place by proprietary AI models to secure user data.
- Businesses that invest in proprietary AI have the potential to create income streams that support

additional development.

- **Control of Quality:** Proprietary AI is subjected to extensive internal testing and optimization, in contrast to open-source models.

8.3.3 Finding a Balance

- A lot of companies, like DeepSeek AI, are implementing a hybrid strategy in which some AI components are open-sourced to promote community contributions but core AI technology is kept proprietary.
- In order to ensure that innovation and security coexist, regulatory frameworks may be extremely important in deciding how AI models are shared.

Accessibility, safety, and ethical issues will all be impacted by the continuous discussion between open-source and proprietary AI.

8.4 AI's Influence on Society

AI is a social revolution with significant ramifications for ethics, human behavior, and international government. It is not only a technical breakthrough. AI systems bring up significant ethical and philosophical issues as they are incorporated into daily life.

8.4.1 AI and Human-AI Cooperation

- **Improving Human Capabilities:** AI enhances human intelligence, allowing for more effective problem-solving in domains such as scientific research, medicine, and law.
- **Ethical AI Decision-Making:** To prevent unforeseen societal repercussions, AI systems must take moral reasoning and ethical considerations into account.
- **Workforce Adaptation:** AI and humans must cohabit in the workforce, necessitating the implementation of strategic policies to handle reskilling and job displacement.

8.4.2 Global Governance and AI

- To avoid abuse, governments and regulatory

agencies must create global guidelines for AI governance.

- Concerns like monitoring, skewed decision-making, and AI-driven disinformation will require ethical standards.

8.4.3 The Philosophical Consequences of AI

- Fundamental queries concerning awareness, free choice, and the nature of intelligence are raised when AI gets closer to reasoning like a human.
- The place of AI in ethical governance, personal autonomy, and decision-making must be decided by societies.

DeepSeek AI is dedicated to developing AI responsibly, making sure that its models address ethical issues and governance obstacles while making a constructive contribution to society.

AI has a bright future, but it also comes with difficult obstacles that need to be carefully considered. The argument over open-source vs proprietary AI, the search for artificial general intelligence (AGI), and the effects of AI on society will all influence how technology develops over the next few decades.

At the vanguard of this development, DeepSeek AI is constantly improving its roadmap to conform to society demands, ethical considerations, and technological breakthroughs. DeepSeek AI can contribute to the creation of a future in which artificial intelligence transforms and fairly benefits humanity by encouraging responsible AI development.

CHAPTER 9

USING DEEPSEEK AI IN REAL-WORLD SITUATIONS

Innovation in a variety of industries is being propelled by the incorporation of Artificial Intelligence (AI) into practical applications. AI is being used by businesses of all sizes, from start-ups to multinational corporations, to increase productivity, make better decisions, and gain a competitive edge. With its sophisticated features, DeepSeek AI offers a flexible platform that lets businesses take advantage of AI's potential in significant ways.

With an emphasis on enterprise-level integration, creating custom AI models, overcoming deployment obstacles, and applications for startups and small enterprises, this chapter examines how DeepSeek AI may be applied in practical settings.

9.1 AI for Small Businesses and Startups

By automating procedures, streamlining operations, and improving customer experiences, artificial intelligence (AI) offers startups and small businesses a chance to compete on an even playing field with their larger rivals. Scalable solutions from DeepSeek AI let business owners innovate without needing a lot of money.

9.1.1 AI's Advantages for Small Businesses

- **Improved Decision-Making:** AI-powered analytics offer practical insights for long-term planning.
- **Automation of Routine Tasks:** Companies can automate marketing, accounting, and customer support processes.
- AI makes it possible to create customized marketing strategies, which enhances consumer retention.

9.1.2 AI Use Cases in Startups

- **Chatbots and Virtual Assistants:** AI-driven chatbots save operating expenses by streamlining customer service.
- **Predictive Analytics for Marketing:** AI systems

examine customer behavior to improve marketing tactics and ad targeting.

- **Supply Chain Optimization:** Demand forecasting powered by AI facilitates effective inventory and logistics management.

9.1.3 AI in Small Business: An Introduction

- Determine the main issues that AI can help with.
- Select affordable AI solutions for automation and insights, such as DeepSeek AI
- Continuously train AI models with relevant business data to increase accuracy.

Startups may use AI to boost output, cut costs, and learn more about their customers all of which will contribute to long-term success.

9.2 Including AI in Enterprise Solutions

AI-driven strategies that can scale across several departments and functions are necessary for larger organizations. DeepSeek AI provides enterprise-level solutions that boost productivity, streamline processes, and stimulate creativity.

9.2.1 Important Domains for AI Integration in Businesses

- **Recruitment and Human Resources**: AI-driven application tracking systems expedite hiring by evaluating resumes and forecasting candidate success.
- **Customer Relationship Management (CRM)**: AI-powered CRM solutions improve client communications by making wise suggestions.
- **Cybersecurity**: AI uses threat intelligence and anomaly detection to identify and stop security breaches.

9.2.2 AI Adoption Case Studies

- **Retail Industry:** A multinational e-commerce business used DeepSeek AI to customize product recommendations, which resulted in a 25% boost in sales.

- **Financial Services:** To improve transaction security and decrease false positives, a financial institution automated fraud detection using AI.

- **Healthcare:** Predictive diagnostics using AI was incorporated into a hospital network, improving patient care by detecting illnesses early.

9.2.3 Best Practices for Enterprise AI Adoption

- **Create a Clear AI Strategy**: Determine the business goals that AI can help with.

- **Assure Data Readiness:** For AI models to function at their best, high-quality, structured data is necessary.

- To encourage adoption and reduce opposition, it is recommended that personnel receive AI literacy training.

AI's revolutionary potential in businesses improves consumer engagement, security, and operational efficiency, laying a solid basis for long-term success.

9.3 Using DeepSeek to Create Custom AI Models

Numerous companies need AI models that are customized to meet their unique requirements. With the help of DeepSeek AI's adaptable platform, businesses may create and implement unique AI models for a range of uses.

9.3.1 Procedures for Creating Personalized AI Models

1. **Define the Problem Statement:** Clearly state the business problem that artificial intelligence is meant to address.

2. **Collect and Prepare Data:** Compile structured, high-quality data pertinent to the goal of the AI model.

3. **Select the Correct AI Algorithm:** Pick from models for natural language processing, machine learning, or deep learning.

4. **Train the AI Model:** Train and adjust the model for accuracy using historical data.

5. **Deploy and Monitor Performance:** Integrate the model into corporate procedures and evaluate its efficacy on an ongoing basis.

9.3.2 Custom AI Model Applications

- **Fraud Detection:** Financial institutions create AI models to instantly spot questionable transactions.
- **Healthcare Diagnostics:** To diagnose diseases early, medical images and patient records are analyzed by custom AI models.
- AI is used in manufacturing quality control to check items on assembly lines for flaws and guarantee quality.

9.3.3 Difficulties in Developing Custom AI Models

- **Data Scarcity:** In order to make accurate predictions, AI models need large datasets.
- **Computational Resources:** Complex model training necessitates powerful computers.
- **Regulatory Compliance**: Businesses like healthcare and finance need to make sure AI solutions adhere to the law.

Custom AI models provide companies specialized

solutions that optimize productivity and creativity in spite of these obstacles.

9.4 Overcoming Obstacles in the Implementation of AI

Even though AI has many benefits, there are a number of obstacles to implementing AI solutions at scale, such as biases in AI decision-making, infrastructural constraints, and ethical issues.

9.4.1 Resolving Scalability Issues

- **Cloud-Based AI Solutions:** Companies can effectively grow AI operations by utilizing cloud services.
- Edge computing boosts real-time AI performance by processing data closer to the source, which lowers latency.
- **Model Optimization:** Using AI models that are lightweight lowers processing needs without sacrificing accuracy.

9.4.2 Reducing Prejudice in AI Systems

- **Representative and Diverse Datasets:** AI models trained on inclusive datasets yield more equitable results.

- **Bias Audits:** Frequent evaluations guarantee AI systems don't perpetuate discriminating tendencies.

- **Human Oversight:** To uphold ethical norms, AI-driven judgments ought to be examined by human specialists.

9.4.3 Building Robust AI Infrastructure

- **Data Governance Frameworks:** Security is improved by establishing explicit guidelines for data collection, storage, and use.

- **AI Regulation Compliance**: Companies are required to abide by data privacy rules like the CCPA and GDPR.

- **Ongoing AI Model Monitoring:** AI systems are kept in line with changing business requirements through frequent updates and retraining.

By overcoming these obstacles, AI implementation will continue to be moral, scalable, and in line with corporate objectives.

Ethical considerations, appropriate infrastructure, and strategic planning are necessary for the successful application of DeepSeek AI in practical settings. AI's revolutionary potential is apparent, whether it is for startups looking to expand, businesses streamlining operations, or organizations creating unique AI models.

Businesses can guarantee AI solutions continue to be efficient, equitable, and advantageous over time by tackling deployment issues like bias, scalability, and data governance. DeepSeek AI keeps giving businesses access to state-of-the-art AI capabilities, opening the door to a more intelligent and effective future.

CHAPTER 10

Conclusion - DeepSeek's AI Revolution

One of the most revolutionary forces in the modern world is artificial intelligence (AI), which is changing industries, redefining human potential, and opening up new avenues for growth. This change has been greatly aided by DeepSeek AI, which has advanced automation, machine learning, and data-driven decision-making.

AI's contribution to society will only increase as it develops further. AI is no longer a sci-fi idea; it is our present and future, from companies streamlining their operations to researchers exploring the limits of artificial general intelligence (AGI). This chapter examines how humans and AI can work together, looks back at the journey thus far, and offers solutions for adjusting to a world driven by AI.

10.1 The AI Journey Thus Far: An Overview of DeepSeek AI's Technological Impact

DeepSeek AI has made a substantial contribution to the AI revolution by providing strong tools that have proved useful across a range of industries. DeepSeek AI has made it possible for developers, researchers, and enterprises to efficiently utilize AI's capabilities, ranging from natural language processing (NLP) to sophisticated data analytics.

10.1.1 Significant Turning Points in the Development of DeepSeek AI

- **NLP Advancements:** DeepSeek AI has transformed human-computer interaction by enabling AI to comprehend, produce, and process human language with previously unheard-of precision.
- **Enhanced Machine Learning Capabilities:** DeepSeek AI gives companies the ability to use machine learning models to automate difficult activities, make data-driven choices, and increase productivity.
- **AI-Powered Creativity:** AI has emerged as a

crucial tool for creative workers, ranging from design automation to content creation.

- **Democratization of AI:** DeepSeek AI has enabled individuals, businesses, and startups to incorporate AI into their processes by lowering the barrier to entry.

10.1.2 DeepSeek AI's Impact on Industries

- **Healthcare:** AI-powered medical imaging analysis, tailored treatment regimens, and diagnostics have led to better patient outcomes.
- **Finance:** AI models have improved risk assessment, algorithmic trading, and fraud detection.
- **Retail and E-commerce:** AI chatbots, automated inventory management, and personalized suggestions have completely changed the way that customers interact with businesses.
- **Manufacturing:** AI-powered quality control and predictive maintenance have lowered costs and improved efficiency.

The impact of DeepSeek AI goes beyond certain sectors; it

is reshaping our digital civilization as a whole.

10.2 AI and Human Cooperation: How AI and Humans Can Cooperate

The question of whether AI will replace human employment or enhance human abilities is one of the most important ones. AI isn't meant to take the place of people; rather, it's meant to augment human potential so that people and organizations may accomplish more.

10.2.1 The Workforce Augmented

- AI is changing employment rather than replacing them. AI is being used in many professions to perform data-intensive or repetitive jobs, freeing up humans to concentrate on more complex decision-making.
- **Doctors and AI:** While AI helps diagnose illnesses more quickly, doctors still offer the personal touch and moral discernment required for patient care.
- **Teachers and AI:** While AI-powered tools aid in personalizing instruction, instructors contribute

mentorship and emotional intelligence.

- **AI and Financial Analysts:** Large volumes of financial data are processed by AI, but human professionals still analyze the data, draw conclusions, and decide on strategies.

10.2.2 Human-AI Synergy: The Best of Both Worlds

- **AI for Efficiency:** AI increases accuracy across a range of fields, streamlines workflows, and automates jobs.
- **People for Creativity and Ethics:** Although AI is capable of producing material, people are still responsible for creativity, ethical judgment, and critical thinking.
- **Working Together to Solve Problems:** Although AI improves research by analyzing data at scale, conclusions are interpreted and used in real-world situations by human professionals.

Together, humans and AI can build a future that combines the finest aspects of both technologies and advances society in ways that neither could on its own.

10.3 Getting Ready for an AI-Driven Future: Adaptation Techniques for People and Companies

Businesses and individuals need to adjust as AI develops further in order to be relevant. To enable responsible AI development, this transition calls for proactive learning, a readiness to adopt new technologies, and ethical considerations.

10.3.1 For Individuals: Developing AI Literacy

- **Learn AI Basics:** In the digital economy, knowing how AI functions will be essential.
- **Build Complementary Skills:** While AI processes data, cognitive abilities such as creativity, emotional intelligence, and critical thinking will always be valuable.
- **Remain Flexible:** The field of artificial intelligence is always changing, thus remaining current requires regular learning.

10.3.2 For Businesses: Embracing AI Transformation

- **Incorporate AI into Business Operations**: Organizations need to investigate how AI may improve productivity, from data-driven decision-making to automated customer service.
- **Invest in AI Training:** To ensure optimal productivity, employees should be trained to collaborate with AI and take use of its possibilities.
- **Make Sure AI Is Used Ethically**: When using AI technologies, businesses must put responsibility, equity, and transparency first.

10.3.3 Ethical Considerations in AI Development

- **Bias and Fairness**: To avoid biased results, AI models must be trained on a variety of datasets.
- **Data Privacy:** In order to safeguard user data, businesses must make sure that regulations are followed.
- **AI Accountability:** Organizations and developers should be accountable for the decisions made by AI and the effects they have on society.

People and companies can properly use AI's potential while guaranteeing long-term growth and sustainability by becoming ready for an AI-driven future.

10.4 Concluding Remarks and Call to Action

Promoting Conscientious AI Development and Application

Amazing prospects are presented by the AI revolution, which is fueled by advancements like DeepSeek AI. It does, however, also present difficulties that call for careful thought and moral accountability.

10.4.1 AI's Future: Prospects and Difficulties

- AI for Social Good: AI may be used to address global problems including healthcare access, education, and climate change.
- **The Risk of AI Misuse:** Robust governance and accountability are necessary to guarantee AI is utilized for moral reasons.
- **AI Policy and Regulation:** To create rules for

responsible AI development, governments and organizations must work together.

10.4.2 A Stakeholder Call to Action

- **For developers:** Create AI systems that are transparent, comprehensible, and fair.
- **For Businesses:** Adopt AI sensibly and inform staff about its implications.
- **Policymakers:** Create rules that strike a balance between creativity and morality.
- **For Individuals:** Keep up with AI advancements and promote responsible AI use.

The decisions we make now, as we lead the AI revolution, will shape AI's place in society in the future. In order to create a world where AI and human intelligence can coexist peacefully, DeepSeek AI and other AI pioneers are constantly pushing the envelope of what is conceivable.

AI has had an incredible journey, and DeepSeek AI has been instrumental in this change. The influence of AI is indisputable, ranging from enabling human-AI collaboration to transforming industries. But enormous power also comes with immense responsibility. A successful AI-driven future depends on careful application, ongoing learning, and ethical considerations.

People and organizations can realize AI's full potential by adopting a collaborative rather than competitive approach. The AI revolution is happening right now, not in the far future. Future generations' worlds will be shaped by how we choose to respond to it.

ABOUT THE AUTHOR

 Author and thought leader in the IT field Taylor Royce is well known. He has a two-decade career and is an expert at tech trend analysis and forecasting, which enables a wide audience to understand complicated concepts.

Royce's considerable involvement in the IT industry stemmed from his passion with technology, which he developed during his computer science studies. He has extensive knowledge of the industry because of his experience in both software development and strategic consulting.

Known for his research and lucidity, he has written multiple best-selling books and contributed to esteemed tech periodicals. Translations of Royce's books throughout the world demonstrate his impact.

Royce is a well-known authority on emerging technologies and their effects on society, frequently requested as a speaker at international conferences and as a guest on tech podcasts. He promotes the development of ethical technology, emphasizing problems like data privacy and the digital divide.

In addition, with a focus on sustainable industry growth, Royce mentors upcoming tech experts and supports IT education projects. Taylor Royce is well known for his ability to combine analytical thinking with technical know-how. He sees a time when technology will ethically benefit humanity.

www.ingramcontent.com/pod-product-compliance
Lightning Source LLC
LaVergne TN
LVHW051705050326
832903LV00032B/4019